LIVING GREEN

Consumable Goods

WORLD
BOOK

a Scott Fetzer company

Chicago

www.worldbookonline.com

Editorial:

Editor in Chief: Paul A. Kobasa
Project Manager: Cassie Mayer
Writer: Brandon Forbes
Researchers: Michael Barr, Jacqueline Jasek
Manager, Contracts & Compliance
  (Rights & Permissions): Loranne K. Shields
Indexer: David Pofelski

Graphics and Design:

Associate Director: Sandra M. Dyrlund
Associate Manager, Design: Brenda B. Tropinski
Associate Manager, Photography: Tom Evans
Book design by: Don Di Sante
Photographs Editor: Kathy Creech

Pre-Press and Manufacturing:

Director: Carma Fazio
Manufacturing Manager: Steve Hueppchen
Production/Technology Manager: Anne Fritzinger

World Book, Inc.
233 N. Michigan Avenue
Chicago, IL 60601
U.S.A.

For information about other World Book publications,
visit our Web site at **http://www.worldbookonline.com** or
call **1-800-WORLDBK (967-5325)**.

For information about sales to schools and libraries, call
1-800-975-3250 (United States), or **1-800-837-5365 (Canada)**.

Picture Acknowledgments:

Front Cover: © Peter Ginter,
Science Faction/Getty Images
© Mark Boulton, Alamy Images 52; © Peter Bowater,
Alamy Images 34; © Ashley Cooper, Alamy Images 27;
© David R. Frazier Photolibrary/Alamy Images 26;
© Digital Vision/Alamy Images 36; © Holt Studios
International Ltd/Alamy Images 33; © Chris Howes,
Wild Places Photography/Alamy Images 30;
© Image Source Black/Alamy Images 25;
© Katharine Andriotis Photography, LLC/Alamy Images 12; © JupiterImages/BananaStock/Alamy Images
20; © Richard Levine, Alamy Images 11; © Mark Lewis,
Alamy Images 10; © Manor Photography/Alamy
Images 26; © NearTheCoast.com/Alamy Images 17;
© Chuck Pefley, Alamy Images 6; © Paul Rapson,
Alamy Images 9; © Helene Rogers, Alamy Images 43;
© Tim Stubbings, Alamy Images 29; © Jim West,
Alamy Images 21; AP/Wide World 11; 15; 35; © Richard
Dunkley, Taxi/Getty Images 35; © Peter Essick, Au-
rora/Getty Images 7; © Jeffrey Hamilton, Digital Vi-
sion/Getty Images 28; Granger Collection 23;
© C.W. McKeen, Syracuse Newspapers/The Image
Works 51; © Jay LaPrete, Bloomberg News/Landov 4;
© Reuters/Landov 50; © Mario Villafuerte,
Bloomberg News/Landov 14; © Xinhua/Landov 54;
© Belinsky Yuri, ITAR-TASS/Landov 22;
© Shutterstock 5, 6, 8, 10, 12, 13, 14, 16, 17, 18, 21, 22, 24,
30, 31, 32, 37, 38, 40, 41, 42, 44, 45, 46, 47, 48, 49, 50,
53, 55, 56, 57, 58, 59.

All maps and illustrations are the exclusive
property of World Book, Inc.

Library of Congress Cataloging-in-Publication Data

Consumable goods.
     p. cm. -- (Living green)
  Includes index.
  Summary: "A guide to living an environmentally friendly lifestyle by changing
general practices at home and making smart choices when purchasing
consumable goods. Explores the harmful impact consumable goods can have
on the environment through the use of natural resources and energy. Features
include fact boxes, glossary, list of recommended reading and web sites, and
index"—Provided by publisher.
  ISBN 978-0-7166-1407-4
  1. Environmental protection--Citizen participation--Juvenile literature. 2. Environmental
protection--Equipment and supplies--Juvenile literature. 3. Consumer goods--Juvenile
literature. 4. Household supplies--Juvenile literature. 5. Consumer education--Juvenile
literature. 6. Green movement--Juvenile literature. I. World Book, Inc.
TD171.7.C68 2009
640—dc22
                                                    2008021469

Living Green
Set ISBN: 978-0-7166-1400-5
Printed in Mexico
1 2 3 4 5 12 11 10 09 08

The text paper of this book contains
a minimum of 10% post-consumer
recovered fiber.

Table of Contents

There is a glossary of terms on pages 60-61. Terms defined in the glossary
are in type **that looks like this** on their first appearance in any section.

Introduction

Modern civilization offers a wide variety of consumable goods.

Every day, we buy and use all kinds of goods, from foods to cosmetics to paper products. Consumable goods are items that can be used for a short period before they are thrown away. Paper towels, light bulbs, batteries, and clothing are a few examples of the many consumable goods found throughout the home. Some consumable goods, such as plastic drink bottles, are thrown away after being used only once.

Trash build-up

Consumable goods harm the environment in many ways. Every piece of trash that is thrown away is either taken to a **landfill**, where it is buried, or to an **incinerator**, where it is burned. In 2006, Americans created 251 million tons (227.7 million metric tons) of trash. Currently, 55 percent of the trash in the United States gets buried in landfills. This amount of trash is so great that more and more landfills have to be created to hold it.

Plastic consumable goods are responsible for a large amount of trash build-up. Plastic is a **synthetic** (human-made) material and takes much longer to **decompose** than natural materials. Plastic items take many lifetimes to decompose in landfills.

Many consumable goods contain substances that can pollute the environment after they are discarded. When these items are buried in landfills, chemicals can seep into the soil and contaminate underground water sources. When they are burned in incinerators, they can release harmful **pollutants** into the air.

Use of natural resources

Natural resources are used to make consumable goods. Trees are cut down so their wood can be used to make paper items. Metal is mined from the ground and used to make food and drink cans. **Petroleum** (also called oil) is drilled from deep underground and used to make plastic consumable items, such as water bottles, food containers, shampoo bottles, toys, and packaging.

Some natural resources cannot be replenished once they are used up, and are therefore called **nonrenewable resources.** Petroleum is a nonrenewable resource that is in very short supply. Forms of petroleum are burned as fuel in vehicles. Petroleum is also burned as fuel to generate electricity at some power plants.

Some natural resources used to make consumable goods, such as trees and plants, are considered **renewable resources.** New plants can be grown to replace the ones that are cut down. However, trees take much longer to grow to their full size than other plants. Many **environmentalists** argue that trees are being cut down faster than they can be replaced.

Trees are a renewable resource, but they take years to reach full size.

Manufacturing bottled water uses fossil fuels, both for the plastic bottles and the energy used in manufacturing and shipping.

Energy use

A huge amount of energy is used in the creation, shipment, and disposal of consumable goods. Most of this energy comes from burning **fossil fuels**, such as coal, oil, and natural gas. Fossil fuels are materials of Earth that can be used as energy to power vehicles, factories, and electric power plants. Fossil fuels are nonrenewable resources, so they cannot be replaced once they are used up.

The life cycle of a plastic drink bottle shows the large amount of energy required to make a consumable good. Petroleum, the material used to make plastic, must be extracted from the ground and shipped to plastic factories. Once the plastic material is made, it is then shipped to another factory, where it is molded and shaped into bottles. The bottles are then filled with water and shipped to stores.

Every step of this process uses energy. The machines that extract the petroleum from the ground burn fossil fuels for energy. The factories that manufacture the plastic material and the water bottles also require energy. Vehicles that transport the bottles to stores burn a form of petroleum for energy.

People use additional energy when they drive to the store to purchase these items. Their cars burn gasoline, which comes from petroleum. When the product is thrown away, trucks, which also burn a form of petroleum, collect the garbage and transport it to landfills. Some trash is transported several hundred miles.

Global warming

Global warming is a major issue associated with energy use. Over the past 200 years, Earth's average surface temperature has continued to increase. Climate change is already endangering many species (kinds) of plants and animals and their **habitats.** It could also increase incidents of drought, famine (prolonged food shortages that lead to hunger and death), and disease in several parts of the world.

Most scientists agree that human activities, particularly the burning of fossil fuels and the clearing of land, are the main cause of global warming. When fossil fuels are burned for energy, gases are released into the atmosphere that trap the sun's heat, much the same way a greenhouse traps heat. Scientists refer to this as the **greenhouse effect.**

Carbon dioxide is the main **greenhouse gas** produced by human activities. It is released into the atmosphere when fossil fuels are burned. The creation, shipment, and disposal of consumable goods are the industries most responsible for the release of carbon dioxide into the atmosphere.

As evidence of global warming has grown, people have sought ways to reduce their **carbon footprint,** or the amount of carbon dioxide **emissions** their individual actions produce each year. Reducing human impact on the environment requires government action, such as laws that set limits for carbon dioxide emissions, but it also involves individual action.

Living green means making choices that benefit people and the environment. There are many ways to live green, from riding a bike instead of driving a car to reducing energy use in the home. Consumable goods are a part of everyday life, but the choices we make in how we buy, use, and dispose of consumable goods can reduce their environmental impact—and our own carbon footprint.

A CLOSER LOOK

Carbon Footprint

The term *carbon footprint* refers to the amount of carbon dioxide released into the atmosphere by an individual or even a consumable good. For example, the average person living in the United Kingdom is responsible for releasing around 10 tons (9 metric tons) of carbon dioxide a year through energy use, while a bag of potato chips releases around 75 grams of carbon dioxide when it is made. You can calculate your own carbon footprint at such Web sites as http://www.carboncounter.org/.

The greenhouse effect

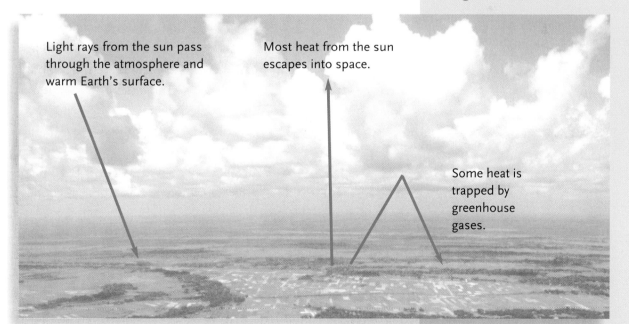

Light rays from the sun pass through the atmosphere and warm Earth's surface.

Most heat from the sun escapes into space.

Some heat is trapped by greenhouse gases.

The Living Room

Section Summary

Light bulbs contribute to home energy use. Switching to energy-efficient light bulbs can help reduce energy use in the home.

Batteries often contain toxic metals. Choosing rechargeable batteries over disposable batteries can help prevent these metals from ending up in landfills.

Toys are often made from natural resources, such as wood, metal, and petroleum. Purchasing used toys or toys made from sustainable materials can help reduce their environmental impact.

LIGHTING

Lighting is responsible for a large amount of wasted energy in the home. One way to save energy is to use lights only when you need them and to turn off lights when you leave the room. A way to save even more energy is by making smart choices when purchasing new light bulbs. There are many types of light bulbs to choose from, and some save more energy than others.

Incandescent light bulbs

The most commonly used light bulb is the **incandescent light bulb.** Incandescent bulbs are very popular because they are cheap, fit many different types of light fixtures, and are sold everywhere. They also give off a warm, far-reaching light that many people prefer to other light bulbs.

Incandescent bulbs work by using an electric current to heat a coil of wire inside the bulb called a **filament.** The filament, which is made from a metal called tungsten, gives off light when the electric current passes through it. The filament gets very hot, which causes incandescent bulbs to give off a lot of heat. In fact, 90 percent of the energy produced by incandescent bulbs is wasted as heat.

Incandescents are the least energy-efficient bulbs available and have the shortest **life span** of any light bulb on the market. They also gradually dim over time. This happens because the tungsten metal that makes up the filament **evaporates** inside the bulb, leaving dark matter which blocks the light.

Compact fluorescent light bulbs (CFL's)

Compact fluorescent light bulbs, or **CFL's**, use less energy than incandescent bulbs. They also generate less heat and last much longer. One CFL bulb can last 5 to 10 years.

CFL's contain three main elements inside their glass tube: a gas, a small amount of mercury (a liquid metal), and phosphor, which is a powder that coats the inside of the tube. When an electric current passes through the tube, microscopic particles (pieces) called **electrons** (negatively charged particles) react with the mercury to release **ultraviolet rays.** These invisible light rays are then absorbed by the phosphor, causing them to glow and give out light.

CFL's are more expensive than incandescent bulbs. However, a person can save around $30 in electricity costs for every incandescent bulb he or she replaces with a CFL.

The biggest drawback to using CFL's is that the mercury inside the glass tube can be harmful to humans and the environment. If they break, protective gloves should be worn when cleaning them up.

Old CFL's should always be taken to a recycling center instead of being thrown in the trash. If CFL's end up in **landfills,** the mercury inside them can seep into the ground and poison nearby water sources.

Choosing compact fluorescent light bulbs can help reduce a household's yearly electricity costs.

Tungsten-halogen light bulbs produce brighter light and last almost twice as long as incandescent bulbs.

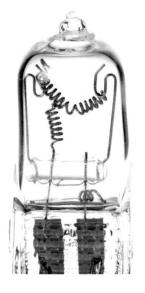

Close-up of a tungsten-halogen light bulb

Tungsten-halogen light bulbs

Tungsten-halogen light bulbs are made of almost all the same components (parts) as incandescent bulbs, but they also contain iodine vapor. This gas prevents the rapid build-up of the dark matter that normally blocks light in incandescent bulbs. Because of the iodine vapor, tungsten-halogen light bulbs produce more light and last almost twice as long as incandescent bulbs.

Tungsten-halogen light bulbs do have some drawbacks. The reaction between the iodine vapor and the tungsten metal creates a lot of pressure and causes the bulb to get extremely hot. This extreme heat can be dangerous if it comes into contact with flammable material. In 1997, famous jazz musician Lionel Hampton lost his home in New York City when a halogen lamp tipped over and caused his bed sheets to catch fire.

Because tungsten-halogen bulbs can become so hot, it is best to use them in enclosed light fixtures where they are out of the way and not in lamps, where they can tip over. They are usually found in patio and outdoor lighting as well as newer indoor fixtures.

Light-emitting diodes (LED's)

One of the newest types of lighting for the home is **light-emitting diodes,** or **LED's.** These lights have been used on computers, stereos, cars, and traffic lights, and are now being fitted for home use.

Unlike incandescent light bulbs, LED's do not use a filament to create light. Instead, they focus electrical energy in one direction from a mineral or metal material through a plastic cover. Because they do not give out light in all directions, many LED's must be grouped in a light fixture to give off the right amount of light. LED's are very small, so this is easily done. LED's can last 50,000 to 100,000 hours and they give off no heat. LED's also will not shatter since they are not made of glass.

Because LED's are so energy efficient, they are also very expensive. Another drawback to LED's is that their light can alter colors in some fabrics.

LED's are used for many common objects, such as traffic signals and walk signs.

A CLOSER LOOK
The Future of Lighting

In the future, lighting may come from tables, walls, curtains, or any surface in the home. Organic light-emitting diodes (OLED's) are devices composed of thin layers of carbon-containing molecules that emit light when electrical energy runs through them. OLED's can work on flat or curved surfaces, and are currently used for cell phone screens, portable digital music players, brake lights, flashlights, and traffic signals, among other items. Scientists are studying ways to adapt OLED's for home use.

Organic LED's may one day become an important part of home lighting.

BATTERIES

Batteries are used to power many items around the home, from alarm clocks to TV remote controls to toys. Batteries come in all shapes and sizes, and most last a short period before they need to be replaced. They spend much more time in landfills, where their metals can seep into the soil and pollute nearby water sources. Reducing your battery waste can help keep these items out of the environment.

Primary batteries

Primary batteries supply power to many small objects, such as toys, remote controls, and flashlights. Primary batteries create power through a chemical reaction that sends electrons from the negative to the positive **terminals** of a battery, which connect to the object that needs power. When the chemicals in a primary battery are used up, the battery becomes useless and is thrown away. Thus, primary batteries are sometimes called **disposable** batteries.

There are several types of primary batteries, all of which use different substances to power them. Alkaline batteries, which are a mixture of an electrolyte (substance that conducts electricity) and different metals, are the most popular type of primary battery. The chart on page 13 lists the common types of primary batteries and their uses.

All batteries should be recycled. They can pollute soil and water when buried in landfills.

Primary batteries used to contain large amounts of mercury, a **heavy metal** that is toxic to humans and the environment. Since 1984, however, battery manufacturers have reduced mercury content in batteries. Most alkaline batteries today use minimal amounts of mercury. Still, primary batteries contain other metals that can pollute soil and enter underground water sources when they are buried in landfills.

Rechargeable batteries

Some primary batteries can be recharged with a device that plugs into an electrical outlet to reverse the flow of electrons from negative to positive, restoring power to the battery. While rechargeable batteries are more expensive than disposable batteries, they save money over their life span. Using 4 rechargeable AA batteries can prevent more than 100 disposable batteries from being thrown away. This saves around $40 and keeps 8 pounds (3.6 kilograms) of hazardous waste out of landfills.

Recycling batteries

When batteries wear out, they should be taken to a place where they will be properly handled, such as a hazardous household materials center. Many schools, libraries, electronics stores, and community centers also collect old batteries for recycling.

Battery recharger

Each type of battery offers advantages and disadvantages that should be considered before purchase.

Types and Uses of Primary Batteries

Disposable	Type/Shape	Advantages	Disadvantages
Alkaline	AA, AAA, C, D, N, 9V	Moderate energy storage; affordable; long shelf life	Energy supply can be drained quickly in high-energy devices or equipment
Lithium	Button, cylindrical	High power output; long shelf life; low temperature performance	High cost; energy supply can be drained quickly in high-energy devices or equipment
Carbon-zinc	AA, AAA, C, D, N, 9V	Low cost; long shelf life	Poor performance at lower temperatures; performance diminishes as power drains from the battery
Air	Button shape	High energy output; long service life	Can operate only in a controlled atmosphere; low power

Critically reviewed by Christopher S. Johnson, Staff Chemist,
Electrochemical Technology Program, Argonne National Laboratory, Argonne, Illinois

The materials and processes used to make toys can have a hidden environmental impact.

TOYS

Toy stores offer a wide selection of items for all ages, from rubber ducks to digital gadgets to remote-controlled cars. Knowing more about the materials used to make toys can help you make smart purchasing decisions for your family and the environment.

Wood toys

Wood is a material used to make a variety of toys, such as building blocks, puzzles, and rolling objects. Wood is a **renewable resource**, and lumber companies often plant new trees to replace the ones they cut down. However, trees take a long time to grow to their full size. In the meantime, young forests do not provide the same diverse **habitat** that old forests give to wildlife. They also absorb less **carbon dioxide** than full-grown trees, leading to more build-up of this gas in the atmosphere.

Metal toys

Such items as toy jewelry, model cars and trains, and other small objects are often made of metal. Metal is a **nonrenewable resource** that must be mined from the ground, a process that strips away soil over large areas of land. The production of metal also uses lots of energy.

Plastic toys

Most toys on the market today are made of plastic, a material that can cause environmental harm in many ways. Plastics are usually made from **petroleum,** a nonrenewable resource that is in very short supply. Plastic is also a non-**biodegradable** material that contributes to trash build-up, so it is important to limit the amount of plastic we throw away.

Green toys

Toys made from environmentally friendly materials are available at some speciality toy stores. "Green" toys often cost more than other toys, so it is worth investigating what steps the company took to reduce their environmental impact. People wishing to buy green toys should look for the following:

- Toys made from renewable materials that can be replenished faster than trees. Examples of such materials include cotton, wool, and bamboo.
- Toys made from materials that have been grown organically. **Organic** farms do not use any human-made chemicals, such as **pesticides** to control bugs or **synthetic fertilizers** to help their crops grow. When these chemicals enter the environment, they can pollute soil and water.
- Toys made from recycled materials, such as plastic, metal, or **reclaimed wood.**
- Toys made from **sustainably** harvested wood. Many of these products bear the Forest Stewardship Council (FSC) logo. The FSC is an international organization that **certifies** wood products that come from well-managed forests.

A CLOSER LOOK
Lead in Toys

Lead is a heavy metal that was once commonly found in paints in the United States. Its use in paint was banned in 1978, after studies indicated that lead could cause brain damage.

Lead has recently been found in paints used to decorate some toys. In 2007, toy manufacturers **recalled** millions of toys that were suspected of having high amounts of lead. These toys were made in factories where safety standards were not being enforced.

Toy stores removed toys that were recalled due to their lead content.

Go Green!

Living green isn't just about the products we buy. It's about instituting environmentally friendly practices at home. Below are some tips to greening your living room.

Using natural light whenever possible can reduce energy consumption. Ceiling fans can help reduce heating and cooling costs.

THE LIVING ROOM

- Use natural lighting as much as possible to reduce energy use. Leave curtains or blinds open during the day to take advantage of natural light.

- Turn off unnecessary lights to save power and make light bulbs last longer.

- Replace incandescent light bulbs with CFL's. This will save hundreds of dollars a year in energy costs and help reduce **greenhouse gas emissions** produced by power plants.

- Install motion sensors, dimmers, and timers to save even more energy. Motion sensor lights turn on when they sense movement. Dimmers and timers can be set to gradually turn down lights that are not in use. They can also be set to turn off lights at a specific time each day to cut down on energy use.

- Use power strips to plug in several lamps and other electrical devices into one power outlet. "Smart" power strips can be set up to keep power from draining to lights and electronic devices when they are not in use.

- Unplug power adaptors and chargers when they are not in use to save money and energy.

- Avoid toys that require disposable batteries.

- Purchase toys at thrift stores or yard sales. Doing so prevents energy from being used to make new toys.

- To keep old toys out of landfills, pass them along to neighbors or younger siblings, donate them to a charity, or bring them to a thrift store.

CFL light bulb

Power strip

Passing along unwanted toys reduces landfill waste and lessens the demand for new toys.

The Kitchen

Section Summary

Cleaning products often contain harmful chemicals. Using cleaners made from natural ingredients can help prevent these chemicals from entering your home.

Paper, plastic, metal, and glass items add to trash build-up in landfills. Reusing and recycling these products can help reduce waste, conserve natural resources, and save energy.

Choosing long-lasting items, such as cloth rags or reusable drink bottles, can also help reduce waste caused by consumable goods in the kitchen.

CLEANING PRODUCTS

Cleaning the kitchen regularly is important for food preparation and cooking. However, many cleaning products contain chemicals that can be more harmful than the mold and bacteria they kill. Choosing the right cleaning products can help prevent **toxins** from harming you and the environment.

Health effects

If you take a look under the kitchen sink, you will likely see the words "caution," "warning," and "danger" written on the packaging of many cleaners. These products contain chemicals that strengthen their cleaning properties, but the chemicals can also be dangerous. **Chlorine** bleach, for example, is a powerful **disinfectant** used in some kitchen and bathroom cleaners that is responsible for many accidental poisonings in the home.

Environmental effects

Substances used to clean the home eventually make their way into the environment. Liquid soaps and cleaners that go down the sink or shower drain are carried through pipes to a **sewage** treatment plant. There, water is cleaned and released into a nearby river or other body of water. Though this water is usually considered safe for water-living organisms, some substances can remain in the water that harm fish and other wildlife.

Phosphates are an example of substances that can cause environmental damage when they are released into bodies of water. Phosphates are used in dishwashing detergents to help break down grease. When phosphates enter a body of water, they can cause a thick layer of algae (small plantlike organisms) to grow on top of the water. **Algal blooms** set off a cycle that eventually uses up oxygen in the water, killing water-living plants and animals.

The table below lists common ingredients found in household cleaners and their potential environmental and health effects.

GREEN FACT

To find out more information about a household cleaner, contact the product's manufacturer and request a Material Safety Data Sheet (MSDS). This sheet lists the product's chemical properties as well as information on health risks, first aid, and storage options.

Common Ingredients in Cleaning Products

Ingredient	Where It's Found	Potential Effects
Ammonia	Floor, glass, and tile cleaners	Poisonous if swallowed; irritates respiratory passages and can cause asthma; can burn skin; made from **petroleum, a nonrenewable resource**
Butyl cellosolve (butyl glycol, ethylene glycol, and monobutyl)	All-purpose cleaners and glass cleaners	Poisonous if swallowed; irritates the lungs
Chlorine bleach (sodium hypochlorite)	Many household cleaners; also sold separately	Irritates the eyes and lungs; can be fatal if swallowed; harms water-living organisms
Diethanolamine (DEA)	Cleaners and detergents	Can produce cancer-causing substances
Monoethanolamine (MEA)	Many cleaning products	Can cause respiratory irritation and asthma; made from petroleum, a nonrenewable resource
Naptha	Glass cleaners; floor and furniture polish	Can cause nausea and headaches
Nonylphenol ethoxylates (NPE's)	Many cleaning products, especially citrus cleaners, detergents, disinfectants, and stain removers	Can break down into toxic substances that harm birds, fish, and mammals
Phthalates	Many cleaning products, especially ones that contain fragrances	Can cause **reproductive** problems in humans and water-living animals
Phosphates	Automatic dishwasher detergents and some laundry detergents	Can reach waterways, where they can kill off plants and animals by contributing to the growth of algal blooms
Sodium hydroxide (lye)	Drain cleaners; metal cleaners; oven cleaners	Can burn skin on contact; irritates the eyes, nose, and throat
Sulfuric acid	Drain cleaners	Can damage eyes, lungs, and skin
Triethanolamine (TEA)	Cleaners and detergents	Can produce cancer-causing substances

Commercial green cleaners

"Green cleaners" are cleaning products made with natural ingredients, such as plant-based substances or castile soap (a hard soap made from olive oil and soda). **Environmentalists** recommend green cleaners because they cause less environmental damage than standard products and are considered safer for human use.

When purchasing green cleaners, it is important to read labels carefully. Many products are labeled "natural," "Earth smart," or "environmentally friendly," but these labels are not **regulated** (controlled) by any government agency and offer no assurance that the company used environmentally safe materials and processes. Nearly all products cause some harm to the environment through their manufacturing, packaging, and shipment. However, products that list specific information, such as the percentage of recycled materials used to make the product, are more likely to have environmental benefits than products that make vague claims.

Cleaning products free of synthetic chemicals have fewer harmful effects on the environment than standard cleaners.

Homemade green cleaners

Taking the time to make homemade green cleaning products can help keep toxic chemicals out of the kitchen. It also reduces the amount of **greenhouse gases** that are released from the packaging and shipment of store-bought cleaners.

Many of the ingredients needed to make cleaners are likely to be found in your home already. White vinegar, for example, is a cooking ingredient that can be used to clean glass, tiles, and kitchen counters.

Baking soda is often used as an ingredient in baked goods, but this mineral-based product also makes a great natural cleaner. Baking soda can reduce bacteria and remove hardened grease and grime. It can also be mixed with other substances to strengthen its cleaning properties. Combined with boiling water and vinegar, baking soda can open up stopped drains. Baking soda mixed with natural soap and water can be used as a gentle cleaner for countertops, floors, and sinks.

The table below lists several ingredients that are ideal for green cleaning. If you do choose to make homemade cleaners, be sure to label them. (For a recipe on how to make an all-purpose green cleaner, see page 56.)

(For a recipe on how to make an all-purpose green cleaner, see page 56.)

GREEN FACT

Grapefruit seed extract is a powerful disinfectant. Several drops of it can be combined with a quart of water and applied to surfaces to kill mold.

Green Cleaning Products

Ingredient	Uses
Baking soda	Surface cleaner; stain remover; odor absorber
Borax*	Mold and mildew remover; odor absorber; clothing whitener *wear gloves when using borax to avoid contact with skin*
Castile soap	General-purpose cleaner
Hydrogen peroxide	Mild bleaching agent; stain remover; disinfectant
Lemon juice*	Grease and stain remover; aluminum, brass, bronze, and copper polishing agent *avoid use on silver*
Tea tree oil	Disinfectant
White vinegar*	Drain opener; deodorizer; disinfectant; stain remover; cleaner for cookware and countertops *avoid use on acetate fibers (often found in tablecloths)*

Many natural ingredients can be combined to make a variety of cleaning products.

PAPER ITEMS

Such products as paper napkins, paper towels, paper bags, and paperboard for food packaging make up a large percentage of consumable goods in the kitchen. Paper products also make up more than 40 percent of the trash in U.S. **landfills.** Choosing environmentally friendly paper products and reducing your own paper waste are two simple ways to green your kitchen.

Making paper

Most paper products are made from wood fibers. At paper mills, wood fibers are separated from wood in a process called pulping. A mixture of water and wood fibers is then dried, flattened, wound into rolls, and shipped to factories that make paper products.

Tissue paper products, such as paper towels and napkins, are also made from wood fibers, but they contain a substance that helps the fibers remain strong when they are wet. Tissue paper products also contain tiny air pockets that help them absorb moisture.

Water and wood fibers are dried, flattened, and wound into rolls of paper.

The amount of wood needed to meet the current demand for paper products is very high. The average person in the United States uses 700 pounds (317.5 kilograms) of paper products each year. For many countries, the process of paper production uses more wood than the amount used to make houses or furniture.

Deforestation

Though agriculture and other industries are largely responsible for forest removal, papermaking has also contributed to **deforestation**. Most paper today is made from **virgin wood fibers** (fibers from newly cut trees). In North America, nearly half the trees that are cut down are used to make paper. Some environmentalists warn that lumber companies are cutting down trees faster than they can replace them.

Papermaking has contributed to deforestation in several parts of North America. In Ontario, Canada, nearly 5.5 million cubic feet (1.55 million cubic meters) of trees from the Kenogami forest are removed each year for lumber and papermaking.

Many paper companies use trees that are grown specifically for papermaking. They also replant trees to replace the ones that are cut down. Thus, some say that papermaking causes minimal damage to the environment. However, environmentalists argue that because the forests planted for papermaking are often **monocultures**, they do not provide the same diverse **habitat** as natural forests. They have only one kind of tree instead of the rich variety of plants found in natural forests.

Scientists warn that the removal of vast areas of forest can disrupt Earth's ecological balance. Not only do forests provide habitats for thousands of species of animals and plants; They also create oxygen and absorb **carbon dioxide**, preventing more of this greenhouse gas from building up in the atmosphere.

A CLOSER LOOK
Making Paper from Rags

Paper has not always been made from wood. The first paper mills in the United States used fibers from old cloth rags. The use of rags for papermaking began nearly 2,000 years ago in China and was also practiced in Europe beginning around 1150 A.D. The use of wood began in the 1800's in the United States because of a rag shortage. Although wood was less easily converted to paper than the fibers from rags, the vast number of trees in the United States made it an appealing alternative.

Workers sorting rags

Even products that say "100 percent recycled" are not necessarily good for the environment.

Green paper products

Making paper from recycled wood fibers can help prevent more forests from being cut down. Recycled paper is used to make a variety of kitchen products, from coffee filters to paper towels and paper napkins.

When purchasing paper products made from recycled content, it is important to read labels carefully. Some products have labels that say "recycled" or "100 percent recycled," but they do not say where the recycled material came from. These products are often made from **pre-consumer waste** content, which includes the pulping waste and paper scraps that are left over from the papermaking process. Pre-consumer waste has always been used to make new paper, so this type of paper does not necessarily have more environmental benefits than regular paper.

Paper mills that use **post-consumer-waste** content take such items as old newspapers, junk mail, and computer printouts and reuse them to make new paper. The Natural Resources Defense Council, an environmental organization based in the United States, recommends that consumers purchase paper made from a high percentage of post-consumer-waste content.

If you wish to purchase paper with the least environmental impact, many environmental organizations recommend choosing re-

Choosing unbleached paper products, such as these coffee filters, can help reduce pollution caused by the bleaching process.

cycled paper items that have been processed without the use of chlorine. Chlorine gas is used to give paper its bright white color, but the process of bleaching paper with chlorine releases harmful **pollutants** into the air.

Paper products that are labeled **"PCF" ("Processed Chlorine Free")** are made from recycled content and have been processed without the use of chlorine, although the recycled fibers may have previously been bleached. The label **"TCF,"** which stands for **"Totally Chlorine Free,"** means the paper was processed without the use of chlorine, but it is not made from recycled content.

Reducing paper waste

Recycled paper products are often more expensive than paper made from virgin wood fibers. However, reducing paper waste at home is an easy way to go green without breaking your budget. Choosing long-lasting alternatives to paper products, such as cloth napkins, towels, and shopping bags, will reduce paper waste and save you money over time.

Recycling is also a key part of reducing paper waste. Unfortunately, many kitchen paper products, such as paper towels or napkins, cannot be recycled. However, you can keep a recycling bin in the kitchen to store other recyclable paper items, such as newspapers, magazines, or computer paper. If your community does not have a recycling program, you can bring paper and other recyclable items to a local recycling center.

Replace paper towels with long-lasting alternatives, such as a cloth towel.

According to some estimates, if every home in the United States bought three fewer rolls of paper towels a year, 120,000 tons (108,862 metric tons) of paper waste would be kept out of landfills and **incinerators.**

PLASTIC ITEMS

The kitchen is a source of a lot of plastic waste. **Disposable** plastic food containers, cups, food wrap, and drink bottles are common kitchen items that are often thrown in the trash. Since most plastics are not **biodegradable,** these items end up clogging landfills. Keeping plastic items out of the trash is vital to living green.

Making plastics

Most plastics are made from petroleum, a valuable **fossil fuel.** Petroleum is processed to form chemical compounds called **synthetic** resins, which are then used to make plastics. Other substances are also added to make plastics stronger, more flexible, or to give them color. Individual plastic items are made in many different ways, but most involve the heating of plastic in order to give it a new shape.

Plastic trash and landfills

Every year, the United States uses about 32 billion pounds (14.5 billion kilograms) of plastic products. Currently, only 2 percent of these products are recycled. This amount of waste means that more fossil fuels have to be used in order to make new plastic items.

Plastic bottled drinks, such as bottled water, make up a large percentage of plastic trash. The United States uses more plastic bottled water than any other country, throwing away an estimated 30 million plastic water bottles every day.

Plastic bags are another major source of plastic trash. Homes in the United States

Plastic bags, which are often used only once, can last many lifetimes in landfills.

throw away around 100 billion plastic bags a year. The majority of these bags comes from small purchases made at stores. Though often used for only 30 minutes, plastic bags can take up to 1,000 years to **decompose** in landfills.

Plastic trash and the oceans

Plastic trash causes large amounts of pollution in the oceans. The **United Nations** Environmental Programme estimates that there are 46,000 floating pieces of plastic garbage for every square mile of ocean in the world. This amount of plastic trash harms wildlife in many ways. Birds, turtles, and other animals sometimes die after eating plastic waste or becoming entangled in it.

Plastic trash from the ocean often makes its way to islands. Below, plastic trash covers the shores of Tuvalu, an island country in the South Pacific.

Health effects

Some plastic items contain chemicals that can move from containers to food and beverages. One such chemical, **bisphenol A (BPA)**, is used in certain kinds of hard plastic water bottles and baby bottles, as well as the lining of some food and drink cans. In 2008, the National Toxicology Program in the United States reported that BPA may be linked to cancer and other health problems. That same year, the Canadian government officially declared BPA to be a toxic substance.

While scientists disagree about the long-term dangers of BPA and other chemicals found in plastics, many feel that more research is needed in order to determine their potential harm. In the meantime, learning about the different types of plastics can help you choose items that are safe for use with food and beverages.

Many plastic food containers and drink bottles contain a number and code that indicate the type of plastic used to make them. The table below lists common types of plastics and their uses.

Some plastic containers may leak harmful chemicals into the food or water they store.

Types of Plastic

Plastic Number	Plastic Type	Common Uses	Comments
1 PETE	PET, PETE (polyethylene terephthalate)	Drink bottles; catsup and salad dressing bottles; peanut butter jars; prepared food trays	Considered safe for use with food and drink, but bottles and containers should not be reused; recyclable
2 HDPE	HDPE (high-density polyethylene)	Juice, milk, and water bottles; detergent bottles; shampoo and cosmetic bottles; yogurt containers; trash bags	Considered safe for use with food and drink; recyclable
3 V	VINYL, PVC (polyvinyl chloride)	Food packaging; detergent bottles; loose-leaf binders; medical tubing	May cause reproductive problems in humans; not recyclable
4 LDPE	LDPE (low-density polyethylene)	Frozen-food bags; produce bags; squeezable bottles; dry-cleaning bags	Considered safe for use with food and drink; recyclable
5 PP	PP (polypropylene)	Catsup bottles; straws; margarine and yogurt containers	Considered safe for use with food and drink; safe for use with microwaves; recyclable
6 PS	PS (polystyrene)	Aspirin bottles; egg cartons; grocery store meat trays; plastic forks and knives; food take-out containers	Can release a suspected cancer-causing substance
7 OTHER	Miscellaneous	Reusable water bottles; some food containers	May contain BPA, a toxic substance; not recyclable

Alternative plastics

Scientists have developed plastics that are made from **renewable resources,** such as corn and soy. These plastics are biodegradable and break down much more quickly than plastics made from petroleum. Some biodegradable plastics take a few years to break down, and others take only a few months. In 2007, scientists from the United States showcased a biodegradable plastic that can break down in salt water within 20 days. This would help prevent many ocean animals from choking on plastic trash.

Though biodegradable plastics are not yet widely used to make consumable goods, they have started to appear on the market. In 2006, a company in the state of Colorado launched Biota, a spring water packaged in biodegradable plastic made from cornstarch.

Reducing plastic waste

Reducing the amount of plastic that ends up in landfills and oceans is an essential part of living green. Purchasing reusable food containers, water bottles, and grocery bags can help reduce your own plastic waste.

When you do use disposable plastic items, be sure to recycle them. Many plastics used in the kitchen can be recycled, which saves energy, reduces pollution, and **conserves** oil. Recycled plastic items can be melted down and made into new goods, such as bottles, carpets, or the stuffing for warm jackets. Recycling just one plastic bottle can save almost half the energy required to make a new plastic bottle.

When recycling plastic, it is important to sort it according to its type. If your community has a recycling program, find out which types of plastic it collects.

Carrying cloth bags

METAL AND GLASS ITEMS

Though paper and plastic make up a large percentage of trash in the kitchen, some waste comes from metal and glass items, such as cans for food and drink.

Metal cans

Metal is a **nonrenewable resource** that is mined from the ground. Most food cans are made of a type of metal called steel, while beverage cans are made of a lightweight metal called aluminum. Every day, people in the United States use 200 million beverage cans and 100 million steel cans.

The production of aluminum and steel requires lots of energy, which makes it very important to recycle these materials. At a recycling plant, aluminum is shredded, melted, and eventually made into new aluminum cans. Steel is recycled in a similar way and can be used to make new food cans, cars, or parts of buildings. Both aluminum and steel can be recycled again and again.

Glass containers

Recycling disposable containers can save large amounts of energy.

Glass is material that is made from sand, limestone, and soda ash. It is used to package such food items as oils, jams, and spices. Some glass items, such as light bulbs and mirrors, cannot be recycled, but most glass items in the kitchen are recyclable.

When glass is taken to a recycling center, it is crushed into tiny pieces called cullet. These pieces are then melted and used to make new glass items, including jars and bottles. Using recycled glass to make new glass uses 40 percent less energy than making glass from new materials.

Most recycling centers ask that glass be sorted by color. You can contact your recycling center to find out their requirements for glass recycling. Prior to recycling, glass items should be rinsed and their caps should be removed.

Go Green!

Reducing waste and limiting the use of harmful chemicals are important parts of living green. Here are some tips to remember when greening your kitchen:

THE KITCHEN

- Take steps to prevent the need for cleaners. Here are a few ways to do so:
  - Wipe down sinks and counters immediately after using them.
  - Layer foil on the bottom of the oven to catch food and grease particles.
  - Use strainers on drains to keep food and grease from clogging pipes.

- Shop with reusable cloth bags to prevent plastic and paper bags from ending up in landfills.

- Check to see if your grocery store accepts used plastic bags and egg cartons for recycling.

- To save money and get the purest water possible without buying bottled water, purchase a water filter. Water filters are sold as refillable pitchers or as an attachment for your faucet.

- For an alternative to bottled drinks, make homemade beverages, such as fruit punch, lemonade, or tea. This will give you more choices for drinks while reducing your plastic waste.

- Use a refillable water bottle to help keep plastic bottles out of landfills.

The Bedroom

Section Summary

Fabrics are made from a variety of materials. Many are made from the cotton plant, which require the use of human-made chemicals to grow. Others are made from plastics, which require the use of petroleum to make. The materials and processes used to make fabrics can cause pollution.

Sustainable fabrics are made in such a way as to reduce their environmental impact. Fabrics made from plants that are grown without the use of chemicals are considered sustainable. Fabrics that are made from recycled materials are also sustainable.

FABRICS

When shopping for clothing, we usually base our purchase decisions on simple factors, such as how the item looks when we try it on and how much it costs. Rarely do we think about how the item was made. However, the materials and processes used to make some fabrics can have hidden environmental costs. Choosing environmentally friendly fabrics for clothing, bed sheets, and other linens is a simple way to green your bedroom.

Cotton

Cotton, which is grown mainly in China and the United States, is the most widely used plant to make fabrics. Many cotton farms use **conventional farming** methods, which include the use of **pesticides** and **synthetic fertilizers.** Pesticides are chemicals that kill insects and fungus that injure plants. Synthetic fertilizers are chemicals that help plants grow. Cotton farming uses only 3 percent of the world's farmland, but it is responsible for about 25 percent of the world's use of pesticides and fertilizers.

Pesticides kill pests that are harmful to plants, such as the boll weevil, but they also kill insects that benefit the plant and surrounding environment, such as honey bees and ladybugs. Pesticides can also damage nearby trees and pollute water sources when they are carried by wind and rainfall.

Like pesticides, synthetic fertilizers can harm waterways. The nutrients in fertilizers can cause too much algae to grow in bodies of water. These **algal blooms** lead to low oxygen levels in the water and causes water-living plants and animals to die.

In addition to the use of pesticides and fertilizers, cotton farms use large amounts of water and often drain local water supplies. In Queensland, Australia, cotton farmers reroute 90 percent of the water from the Darling River to their crops. The **United Nations** has reported that an average of 660 gallons (2,500 liters) of water is needed to make just one cotton shirt.

These sheep are being dipped in pesticides.

Wool

Wool, which comes from sheep and other animals, is a fiber commonly used to make sweaters and blankets. Most wool comes from conventional farms, where sheep are regularly dipped in pesticides to prevent disease from pests. In addition to the environmental damage they can cause, pesticides are also poisonous to humans. Some sheep farmers in the United Kingdom have reported flulike symptoms that are associated with pesticide exposure.

Fur

Every year, more than 50 million animals are hunted, killed, and skinned for their fur. Besides the damage to animal populations, this process uses large amounts of **fossil fuels** for energy. Raising farm animals requires energy for their feed and care. The processing and shipment of fur uses additional energy.

Synthetic fabrics

Beginning in the 1940's, clothing makers began to use synthetic fabric alternatives to cotton, wool, and fur. Polyester, nylon, acrylic, and other materials were developed in laboratories. The production of these fabrics is energy-intensive and involves the use of potentially harmful chemicals.

Most synthetic fabrics are made from plastic, a non-**biodegradable** material that causes large amounts of trash to build up in **landfills.** Another drawback to plastic is that it is made from **petroleum**, a valuable fossil fuel. As you have read, fossil fuels are **nonrenewable resources.**

Additional fossil fuels are used as energy to make synthetic fabrics, which releases **carbon dioxide** into the atmosphere. Overall, it takes more energy to make synthetic fabrics than natural fabrics. Polyester, a common synthetic fabric, takes 67 percent more energy to make than cotton.

Synthetic fabrics also contain chemicals that may cause health problems. The chemical **formaldehyde** (*fawr MAL duh hyd*) is added to many synthetic fabrics to prevent wrinkling and to help them hold their shape. However, formaldehyde can irritate the eyes, nose, and throat, and has been shown to cause cancer in laboratory animals. It can also trigger asthma and allergies.

Polyester threads are made from plastic in factories.

Sustainable fabrics

The flax plant requires less energy to grow than cotton.

Many companies sell clothing, bed sheets, and other linens that are made from **sustainable** materials. Sustainable fabrics are made from plants and animals that are grown or raised in a way that **conserves** natural resources and prevents harmful chemicals from entering the environment. Clothing made from recycled materials, such as plastic drink bottles, is also considered sustainable.

Hemp and flax plants are often used to make sustainable fabrics. The hemp plant is naturally resistant to insects and has strong fibers that can be used to make a variety of items, such as ropes and paper products. Linen fabrics are made from the flax plant, which is also resistant to insects and takes less energy to produce than cotton.

Cotton and wool that have been harvested organically are also considered sustainable materials. To be listed as **organic**, a crop must be grown in fields where chemical pesticides and fertilizers have not been used for at least three years. Organic wool comes from sheep raised without the use of synthetic chemicals.

Consumer demand for organic fabrics has created a market for sustainable clothing. These items are often more expensive than clothing made from conventional fabrics, but they often have less of an environmental cost.

A CLOSER LOOK
Fabric Dyes

Many fabric dyes contain toxic chemicals and **heavy metals** that can be harmful to people and the environment. Textile (fabric) companies in some countries dump wastewater from fabric dye production into nearby rivers and streams, killing fish and other wildlife.

Some clothing manufacturers use alternative fabric dyes to minimize their environmental impact. Fiber-reactive dyes are made from synthetic chemicals. They contain no heavy metals or known toxic substances and create less wastewater than standard dyes. Dirt dyes use minerals and irons to give clothing its color, while color-grown cotton cuts out the need for dyes altogether. It is naturally colored and comes in such colors as brown, green, and red.

Go Green!

Making smart decisions when purchasing clothing and bedroom linens can help reduce their impact on the environment. Here are additional tips to greening your bedroom.

THE BEDROOM

- Avoid purchasing clothing made from fabrics that need to be dry cleaned, such as silk. Dry cleaning is an effective way to clean delicate fabrics, but it involves the use of toxic chemicals, which can enter the environment.

- For clothing you already own that requires dry cleaning, look for "green" dry cleaners that use environmentally friendly processes.

- Before purchasing clothes, check the stitching and fabric to make sure they are well made. Though often more expensive than clothing sold in chain stores, well-made clothing usually lasts longer and saves money over time.

- Buy clothes that can be easily repaired and won't go out of fashion quickly so you will not have to buy new clothing as often.

- Whenever possible, wear clothes more than once before washing them. This will help save energy and water.

Don't throw away old clothing items. Instead, give them to younger siblings, resale stores, or charity. You can also buy used clothing whenever possible.

The most environmentally friendly clothing is the clothing you already own. Try to make your clothes last as long as possible to conserve the use of energy and materials needed to make new clothes. Here are a few ways to keep old clothes going:

- Wash clothes in cold water. This helps them keep their colors and uses less energy than hot water.
- Use a damp cloth to remove dirt and other marks from clothing before they are washed. This may prevent the need to wash it.
- Sew patches onto clothes that have holes. These can be put on the inside of the clothes to hide the repair.
- Cut long pants that have holes in the knees into shorts.
- Reuse old clothes as towels, cleaning rags, or as fabric to repair other clothing.

If you have access to a sewing machine, you can learn to make your own clothes. Fabric stores sell patterns for a wide variety of clothing styles. You can also make such items as pillow covers, drapes, and bags.

Simple repairs and alterations can help you get the most out of the clothes you already own.

The Bathroom

Section Summary

Personal-care products and their packaging are often made from petroleum, a nonrenewable resource.

The chemicals in some personal-care products can cause allergies, skin irritations, or more serious health problems.

In order to avoid harmful chemicals in personal-care products, read ingredient labels and look for products that have been certified by outside parties. You can also make some products at home.

Many cosmetics and their packaging are made from petroleum.

PERSONAL-CARE PRODUCTS

Personal-care products include shampoos, soaps, make-up, lotions, and other items commonly found in the bathroom. These products often contain appealing fragrances and packaging to entice consumers to buy them, but there is growing concern about the substances used to make them and their effects on people and the environment.

Environmental effects

Many personal-care products are made from **petroleum,** a valuable **nonrenewable resource.** These items often come with plastic packaging, such as a compact case or liquid soap container, which is also made from petroleum. Packaging materials are usually thrown in the trash once the item is used up, contributing to waste in **landfills.**

Health effects

Personal-care products, especially petroleum-based items, often contain chemicals that can cause minor health problems, such as allergies and skin irritations. However, some chemicals used in these products are suspected of causing more serious health problems when used over long periods.

In the United States, information about the safety of cosmetic ingredients is available for only 11 percent of the 10,500 ingredients used. The **European Union** has much stricter standards, and requires that manufacturers prove their ingredients are safe before they can sell products that contain them.

Many scientists argue that the amount of chemicals found in personal-care products is too small to cause any health problems. Others say that because these products are used every day, their chemicals can build up in people's bodies over time. The chart below lists some of the ingredients found in personal-care products and their potential health effects.

Ingredients in Personal-Care Products

Ingredient	Where It's Found	Harmful Effects
1,4 Dioxane (present in ingredients ending with –eth)	Shampoos; children's bubble bath products	Known cancer-causing substance
Coal tar colors (FD&C Blue 1, Green 3, Yellow 5 & 6; D&C Red 33)	Hair color; make-up products	Known cancer-causing substances
Diethanolamine (DEA)	Body wash and body cleansers; foundation; after shave; mascara; sunscreen and tanning oils	Suspected cancer-causing substance
Formaldehyde (formalin)	Nail treatments; blush and face powder	Known cancer-causing substance; may cause an allergic reaction over time
Fragrances (parfum)	A variety of products (cleansers, moisturizers, make-up)	May cause irritation to eyes and respiratory tract
Nonoxynol or nonylphenol ethoxylate	Hair care products; hair dyes	Can cause **reproductive** problems
Parabens (methyl-, ethyl-, propyl- and butyl-parabens)	Liquid hand soap; conditioner; facial cleanser; toothpaste; shaving cream	Can affect the endocrine system, which **regulates** various body functions
Phenylenediamine	Hair dyes	Suspected cancer-causing substance
Phthalates (DEHP, DHP, and DBP5 (not identified on cosmetic labels when they are in the fragrance)	Soaps; shampoos; nail polish; perfume; hair sprays	May cause reproductive or developmental problems
Triclosan	Acne treatment; antiperspirants and deodorants; facial cleansers; liquid hand soaps; lip products; facial moisturizer	Can cause eye and skin irritation; may promote antibiotic resistance; may form human cancer-causing substances in chlorinated water

Green personal-care products

As the demand for safer toiletries and cosmetics has grown, more companies are offering products made from natural ingredients, such as plant oils. However, traces of harmful chemicals have been found in some products that claim to be green. In 2008, tests of 100 personal-care products that were labeled "natural" or "**organic**" revealed that nearly half of them contained the chemical 1,4-dioxane, a suspected cancer-causing substance.

Some products have labels to show that they have been **certified** (reviewed and approved) by outside parties, such as the United States Department of Agriculture (USDA). Many cosmetic companies have signed the Compact for Safe Cosmetics, a volunteer agreement to keep harmful ingredients out of cosmetics. You can view a list of such companies at www.safecosmetics.org.

The table at the bottom of this page lists a few organizations that certify cosmetic products.

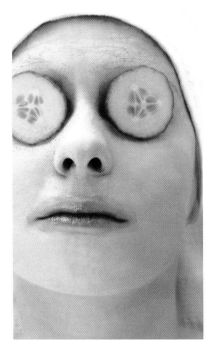

Facial masks can be made at home from herbs, fruits, and vegetables.

Homemade personal-care products

One way to keep harmful chemicals out of your personal-care products is to make your own. A variety of natural herbs, fruits, and vegetables can be combined to create moisturizing lotions, facial cleansers, and hair dyes that are cheaper than store-bought goods. Strawberries and cucumbers can be crushed and used to moisten skin. Herbs such as lavender, sage, and thyme can be used to make body scrubs.

Organizations that Certify Cosmetic Products

Label	What It Means
BDIH* *Federation of German Industries and Trading Firms	Natural ingredients were used in the product whenever possible; the product is free of petroleum-based ingredients and **synthetic** dyes and fragrances; animals were not used for product testing.
Ecocert's* "Eco" Label *An organic certification organization based in France	At least 95 percent of the ingredients are natural; at least 50 percent of the vegetable-based ingredients are certified organic; at least 5 percent of the ingredients in the finished product are certified organic. Products that bear Ecocert's "Bio" label meet even higher standards.
Leaping Bunny* *Created by the Coalition for Consumer Information on Cosmetics, a U.S.-based organization	Product development did not involve animal testing.
USDA Organic	Product was made with organic ingredients.

Go Green!

Many people use a wide range of personal-care products that last a short period before their packaging ends up in the trash. Here are a few ways to green your bathroom by reducing waste from these items:

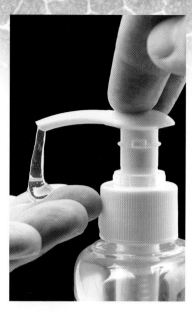

THE BATHROOM

- Choose products that will last as long as possible, such as a reusable eye shadow holder.

- Use a bar of soap instead of body wash in the shower. Soap bar packets are cheaper than body wash, do not come in a plastic container, and tend to last longer.

- You can avoid packaging waste altogether by making some personal-care products at home. Here a few natural cosmetic alternatives to store-bought goods:
  - Milk and honey can be combined to sooth and moisturize dry skin.
  - Sugar, salt, and baking soda can be used as a face scrub.
  - Clay and mud can help clear out pores when applied as a face mask.
  - Herbal bath bags can be made by combining oatmeal, salt, and a selection of herbs. (For instructions on how to make an herbal bath bag, see page 58.)

Herbs and vegetables can be combined to create lotions and cleansers.

The Laundry Room

Section Summary

Laundry products, such as cleaning detergents, fabric softeners, and whiteners, help keep our clothing clean and fresh. However, these products often contain chemicals that can have unexpected environmental and health effects. To green your laundry practices, purchase laundry products that are made from natural ingredients.

LAUNDRY PRODUCTS

Laundry products are used to clean, soften, and whiten clothes and other linens. Knowing more about the substances used to make these products is the first step to doing green laundry.

Detergents and fabric softeners

Laundry detergents often contain chemicals that help strengthen their cleaning properties, but these chemicals can harm fish and wildlife when they enter the environment. Water used by washing machines travels through pipes to a **sewage** treatment plant, where it is cleaned and eventually released into bodies of water. However, some chemicals remain in the water even after it is treated. **Synthetic surfactants**, for example, are chemicals used in laundry detergents that have been found in some freshwater sources. They have been shown to cause genetic changes in fish.

Most laundry detergents and fabric softeners contain **synthetic** fragrances that make laundry smell fresh. However, the chemicals used in these fragrances can cause allergies and irritate the eyes and skin. These products also contain phtha- lates, which are chemicals that help preserve fragrances. Some studies suggest that prolonged exposure to phthalates may cause **reproductive** disorders in humans.

Whiteners

Chlorine bleach is a toxic substance that is sometimes used to whiten clothes. It is an irritant to the eyes, nose, and throat, and can be fatal if swallowed. Chlorine bleach can also harm fish and other wildlife when it enters freshwater sources.

Green laundry products

Those wishing to green their laundry practices should look for detergents made from all-natural soaps or vegetable-based ingredients. For eco-friendly fabric softeners, choose ones that are vegetable-based. To get your whites bright, choose clothing whiteners free of chlorine bleach.

Drying laundry on a clothesline saves both energy and money.

Go Green!

Choosing green laundry products can help keep you and the environ- ment healthy. Here are some tips to greening your laundry:

THE LAUNDRY ROOM

- Read laundry detergent labels closely to see what chemicals they contain. Labels such as "natural" or "nontoxic" do not always mean that products are free of harmful chemicals.

- Buy large packages of concen- trated detergent to cut down on packaging trash.

- Wash clothes in cold water. Washing machines use more energy and therefore produce more **carbon dioxide** when they use hot water.

- Line dry as many clothes as possible. This helps reduce carbon dioxide **emissions** that are produced by dryers.

- Make some laundry products at home. To soften clothes, add half a cup of baking soda to the rinse cycle of your wash. To whiten clothes, add half a cup of hydrogen peroxide to the rinse cycle.

The Office

Section Summary

Office paper products contribute to large amounts of paper waste and are often made with chemicals that can cause pollution. Choosing paper products that are made from recycled content and are chlorine-free can help reduce paper's environmental impact.

Writing and drawing utensils contribute to waste in landfills. Writing implements that are refillable and made with sustainable materials are more environmentally friendly than disposable writing implements.

PAPER PRODUCTS

The tasks we perform at home, work, and school often involve the use of paper. Reducing paper waste and recycling the paper we use are important practices for living green. Learning more about the types of paper available is an additional way to green your paper use. (For a complete discussion of paper and its environmental effects, see pages 22-25.)

Recycled paper

Though most computer paper is made from **virgin wood fibers** (fibers from newly cut trees), some companies make office paper from recycled content. These products are more expensive than paper made from virgin wood fibers, but they help **conserve** forests and use less energy in their production.

As with kitchen paper products, computer paper made from a high percentage of **post-consumer-waste** content, such as old newspapers or used computer paper, is the greenest option. Some companies sell additional office paper items that are made from post-consumer-waste content, such as envelopes, note pads, and self-stick notes.

Some paper products are made from **pre-consumer waste**, and are therefore advertised as recycled paper. However, pre-consumer waste includes materials that have always been reused in the papermaking process, such as wood scraps from paper mills. It does not include paper already used by people, so it has less of an environmental benefit than post-consumer-waste paper.

Chlorine-free paper

Most computer paper gets its white color by being bleached with **chlorine** gas. When this gas combines with wood pulp, **toxins** are released that too often find their way into the environment through contact with water at a paper mill or by being buried in a **landfill**.

For more environmentally friendly paper, choose paper that has been processed without the use of chlorine. Products that are labeled "**PCF**" ("**Processed Chlorine Free**") have been made from post-consumer waste content and were processed without the use of bleach. "**Totally Chlorine Free**" ("**TCF**") is a label used for paper products that are processed without the use of bleach but have no recycled content.

Alternative papers

A few paper companies are now using the fibers from hemp and kenaf plants to make paper. Hemp plants have strong fibers that are excellent for paper production. Kenaf is a cottonlike plant that is grown mainly in China, Bangladesh, Thailand, and Myanmar. Both kenaf and hemp can be grown faster than trees and take up far less land.

Although **environmentalists** have praised the benefits of hemp and kenaf, both materials are currently expensive alternatives to wood-based paper. Some specialty papers made of hemp are available in the United States, and a few companies have begun to print their catalogs on hemp paper. If products made from these materials grow in popularity, their cost could come down.

Inkjet printer cartridges

WRITING AND DRAWING UTENSILS

Every day, people of all ages use writing and drawing utensils, from pens and pencils to markers and crayons. Most writing and drawing utensils are made from natural resources and last only a short period before they are thrown in the trash. Choosing utensils that are made from **sustainable** materials can help minimize their environmental impact.

Traditional pencils

Computers have replaced the need for a lot of handwriting, but pencils are still widely used throughout the world. Traditional pencils are made of wood and graphite, a mineral that is mined from the ground. The graphite makes up the writing core of the pencil and is commonly called lead, though it has no relation to the **heavy metal** called lead.

Pencils made from recycled wood or paper are now available in office-supply stores. Some companies even make recycled pencils from such materials as old currency (money), cardboard, and blue jeans.

Mechanical pencils

Mechanical pencils have a lead writing core that is contained within a metal or plastic case. Unlike traditional pencils, mechanical pencils are reusable. Packs of lead can be purchased to refill the pencil when the lead runs out. However, mechanical pencils are often made from **nonrenewable resources.** Their cases add to waste at

Some traditional pencils are now made from recycled wood or other materials.

landfills and can release harmful **pollutants** when burned in an **incinerator.**

A few companies make mechanical pencils from such recycled materials as car headlights, compact discs, plastic shopping bags, and **reclaimed wood** from furniture manufacturers. These products are sold at some office-supply stores and specialty Web sites.

Pens

Like mechanical pencils, most pens have plastic or metal cases that can cause environmental harm when they are thrown in the trash. Some companies now offer pens made out of recycled plastic soda bottles, milk jugs, and detergent containers. There are even **biodegradable** pens made from such materials as corn.

While pencils use graphite to make their marks, pens use ink. Many pens available today are made from water-based inks, which have few harmful substances. These pens are often labeled "nontoxic" and are considered safe for human use. Refillable pens are also available at stores and cost the same as **disposable** pens. Some refillable pens are even made from recycled materials.

Water-based inks are now commonly used in pens and have few harmful substances.

Markers

Markers come in a variety of types to suit different purposes, such as coloring pictures or highlighting text. Water-based markers are the most environmentally friendly, although some dyes used in water-based markers can cause allergic reactions or asthma.

Permanent markers leave long-lasting marks, and are often used for labeling items. These markers use inks that contain chemical compounds called **volatile organic compounds (VOC's)**. VOC's can

Some markers release fumes that can cause nausea, dizziness, and headache.

cause nausea, dizziness, headache, and irritation of the eyes, nose, and throat. When you do need to use permanent markers, keep your head far from the pen to limit your exposure to these toxic fumes.

When purchasing markers, look for ones that are labeled "nontoxic." You can also check the label to see if they have been **certified** by an outside party. The Art and Creative Materials Institute (ACMI) is an organization based in Massachusetts that reviews pens, markers, and other materials to assure that they are safe for human use. The ACMI's AP (Approved Product) seal means that ACMI's team of scientists did not find the product to have toxic materials in quantities large enough to affect the health of adults and children. You can view a list of ACMI-certified products at www.acminet.org.

Crayons

Most crayons are made by adding pigments (coloring materials) to paraffin wax, a material that is usually made from **petroleum**. However, some companies have begun to make crayons that use soybeans as a substitute for paraffin wax. Many environmentalists consider soybeans a sustainable alternative to petroleum because they are plants that can be grown quickly.

Go Green!

Here are some important tips and things to remember about consumable goods in the office.

THE OFFICE

- Reduce paper waste by reusing old paper. Keep old printouts and envelopes to use as scrap paper for notes or lists. You can also print on the back of one-sided printouts.

- Set your printer to print on both sides of the paper.

- Read articles and view pictures on your computer monitor so you don't have to print them out.

- Purchase writing implements that use minimal packaging or that come in packaging made from recycled materials.

- Buy large packs of pencils and pens to reduce trash from packaging.

- Keep caps on pens and markers to keep them from drying out.

Reusing and recycling paper can greatly reduce office waste.

The Yard

Section Summary

Fertilizers and pesticides are human-made chemicals that are used to help plants grow and keep pests away. However, these chemicals can pollute soil and water.

You can avoid the use of chemicals in your yard by taking a more active role in gardening, such as removing insects from plants by hand.

Synthetic fertilizers can cause algal blooms that kill fish and other wildlife.

FERTILIZERS

Fertilizers supply extra nutrients to such yard plants as flowers, shrubs, and grass. Though the chemicals in fertilizers can help plants grow, they can also cause environmental damage that lasts much longer than a garden's blooms.

Synthetic fertilizers

Synthetic fertilizers, also called inorganic fertilizers, are made from chemicals and are commonly used on yard plants and for **conventional farming.** The mining and processing of the raw materials needed to make synthetic fertilizers can harm the environment. Many minerals used in making fertilizer are dug from the earth in open-pit mines, which often leave large areas of stripped land on which few things can grow.

Rainfall can cause the minerals in synthetic fertilizers to enter rivers, lakes, and streams. When these minerals build up in waterways, they can create **algal blooms,** which eventually lead to reduced oxygen levels in the water. This process creates areas in the water called **dead zones,** where no plants and animals can survive. Each year, a dead zone the size of New Jersey appears in the Gulf of Mexico. This area is caused by the build-up of synthetic fertilizers that make their way down the Mississippi River and eventually into the Gulf.

Organic fertilizers

Organic fertilizers give plants the nutrients they need with minimal environmental impact. Organic fertilizer is made of **decomposed** plant matter or animal waste. A selection of organic fertilizers is often available at home-supply and garden stores.

The greenest way to fertilize plants is by creating your own organic fertilizer through **composting.** Composting is a process where leaves, food scraps, grass clippings, and yard waste are combined in a pile and left to decompose for several weeks. These substances eventually turn into a rich fertilizer full of nutrients for growing plants. The compost pile is turned with a pitchfork or shovel every two weeks so that newer waste can break down more quickly.

Many stores sell compost bins, which are barrel-shaped containers that make it easier to turn over the compost and keep the decomposing materials away from animals and insects. For city dwellers, very small compost bins are available that can be kept in the kitchen. These generally make enough compost to feed houseplants and small gardens.

While it takes time to produce enough compost for a garden or a yard, composting is a great way to recycle food waste from your kitchen and keep synthetic fertilizers from polluting water sources.

Composting can reduce landfill waste and produce organic fertilizer for gardens.

PESTICIDES

Pesticides are commonly used to kill unwanted pests in the backyard. Even though pesticides are poisonous, many people purchase them because they are effective and easy to use. In the United States alone, at least 90 million pounds (41 million kilograms) of pesticides are spread around homes each year.

Health risks

Pesticides can be very dangerous for people and animals. Children are especially vulnerable to the chemicals used in many pesticides. Working over the past 30 years, researchers in Mexico have discovered that young children exposed to pesticides have lower imagination and intelligence levels than children who grow up without exposure to pesticides. Some studies have shown that pesticides can cause birth defects. They have also been linked to breast cancer.

Around the home, pesticides are easily tracked indoors from the yard on shoes or by pets. Dogs living in homes that use pesticides are twice as likely to develop cancer.

Integrated pest management

Integrated pest management (IPM) is a green way to manage weeds, insects, and rodents in the yard. IPM involves more active participation by people. **Mulching** patchy areas of lawn to keep down weeds, picking harmful insects and their eggs off plants by hand, and planting yellow flowers to attract beneficial insects are a few examples of ways to use IPM. While IPM requires more effort than using pesticides, it keeps dangerous chemicals out of the yard while teaching the basic principles of agriculture.

Integrated pest management methods can keep plants pest-free without the use of chemicals.

Go Green!

The yard is a place where people can enjoy the outdoors with the conveniences of home. Here are tips to keeping the yard safe for your family and the environment:

THE YARD

- Avoid using combination fertilizer-pesticide products. A chemical used in these products, called 2,4-D, has been linked to cancer and can make humans and animals sick.

- Plant strong-smelling herbs and spices in your garden to help keep pests away. You can also spray plants with a spoonful of cayenne pepper mixed with water to ward off harmful insects.

- Water the lawn and garden plants early in the morning. This prevents water from **evaporating** during the hottest part of the day.

- Use a rotary lawn mower (hand-powered mower) instead of a gasoline-powered mower. Gasoline mowers emit large amounts of air **pollutants**.

Pulling weeds by hand and using a rotary lawn mower can reduce pollution.

- Keep grass at least 3 inches (7.6 centimeters) high when you cut it. Researchers have found that mowing grass high is a natural way to keep weeds away without the use of pesticides.

Taking Action

Section Summary

Governments around the world have passed laws to protect natural resources and encourage environmental responsibility.

Businesses are working toward creating environmentally sound practices. These include the establishment of recycling programs and investment in renewable energy sources.

Individuals can help reduce the environmental impact of consumable goods by encouraging businesses and governments to set higher environmental standards for these products.

Leaders of the European Union meet every year to discuss new energy policies and climate change.

Government regulation

In recent years, governments around the world have passed laws to protect natural resources and encourage environmental responsibility.

In the United States, the **Environmental Protection Agency (EPA)** and state governments have helped enforce and continually update important environmental laws, such as the Clean Air Act of 1963 and the Clean Water Act of 1972. These pieces of legislation were passed by the U.S. Congress to establish environmental standards relating to air and water pollution.

In 2008, the **European Union** worked toward implementing a sweeping climate change reform treaty. The treaty will reduce **carbon dioxide emissions** and cut taxes on green goods so more people can afford them.

Some acts have targeted the disposal of consumable goods. Since 1989, 13 U.S. states have passed laws to encourage consumers to recycle batteries. Many states have also banned the burning of batteries in **incinerators** and the disposal of batteries in **landfills.**

While governments have taken environmental responsibility

seriously, they could do much more to protect the environment. Citizens can help by learning about the importance of living green so they can influence their leaders to pass laws that help to create a **sustainable** world.

Green businesses

Some businesses and corporations are working toward creating environmentally sound practices. Many have created mandatory (required) recycling programs for their offices. Others pay **carbon offsets** to balance the carbon dioxide emissions they create. Carbon offsets allow companies to direct money toward a program that will help reduce carbon emissions in some way, such as investing in **renewable** energy sources or planting trees.

Some corporations have met with others in the same industry and made agreements to be environmentally responsible. More than 600 global companies have signed the Compact for Safe Cosmetics, which is a promise to remove harmful substances from cosmetic products.

Internationally, environmental responsibility is recognized at the World Economic Forum, a meeting between major governments of the world to discuss financial matters. Each year at this meeting, a list of the Top 100 Green corporations is released. This list includes companies that save large amounts of energy or work toward fighting pollution in some way.

Individual action

Most businesses do not simply decide to go green. Rather, they respond to a rising call from customers to take environmental responsibility seriously. Here are three ways you can do more to reduce the impact of consumable goods on the environment:

1. Know the environmental practices behind the products you buy.
2. Share this knowledge with family and friends.
3. Participate in campaigns that encourage businesses and governments to set higher environmental standards for consumable goods.

In 2007, the computer company Dell launched the Plant a Tree for Me program to help offset the impact of electricity used by computers. Tree-planting programs aim to reduce a company's **carbon footprint.** They do so by planting more forests to absorb excess carbon dioxide that results from energy use. Dell partnered with the Conservation Fund and Carbonfund.org (two U.S.-based non-profit organizations) to plant trees in sustainable forests. Computer users who make a small donation can help fund the planting of trees.

Recipes and Activities

Try the recipes and activities on the next few pages to learn how to make consumable goods from materials around the house.

NATURAL ALL-PURPOSE CLEANER

Introduction
This natural cleaner is safe for use on nearly every surface of the house. Try using it on kitchen counters, bathroom tile, or to wipe down sinks.

Materials:
- 36-ounce plastic spray bottle
- Water
- Natural dishwashing soap
- Selection of essential oils (oils that can be used as a fragrance)

Directions:
1. Fill the plastic spray bottle almost to the top with water.
2. Add 1 teaspoon of natural dishwashing soap or another natural all-purpose cleaner.
3. Add 1 teaspoon of any natural essential oils you have. Good oils to choose for cleaning include lemon, cinnamon, clove, and spruce.
4. Shake the cleaning mixture well before using. Now you have an all-natural cleaner to use around the house!

NATURAL DRAIN CLEANER

Introduction

Natural drain cleaners can be used to clear simple clogs caused by soaps or other materials. If this drain cleaner doesn't unclog your sink or shower drain, it may be time to call a plumber.

Materials:

- 1 cup white vinegar
- 4 tablespoons baking soda
- Tea kettle for boiling water
- Drain cover or small plate

Directions:

1. Make sure all of the water clogging the drain has gone down the drain and all hair or other build-up is cleaned out as far as you can see.
2. Fill a tea kettle with water and bring it to a boil.
3. Pour 4 tablespoons of baking soda down the drain, followed in quick succession by 1 cup of white vinegar and then boiling water.
4. Immediately cover the drain with a drain cover (if you don't have one, a small plate will work). Leave the drain covered for 30 minutes. When you remove the cover, your drain should now be unclogged. If not, repeat once more.

HERBAL BATH BAG

Introduction

Although taking a bath uses more water than taking a shower, there are times when we need a soak in the tub to relieve aches and pains. Adding an herbal bath bag to your bath can create a soothing environment for your bath.

Materials:

- ½ cup herb mixture
- ¾ cup oatmeal
- 2 tablespoons salt
- Piece of cheesecloth measuring 12 by 12 inches (30.5 by 30.5 centimeters)
- String

Directions:

1. Select some of your favorite herbs from your garden or the store. These can include sage, rosemary, thyme, lavender, rose petals, or even orange peels.
2. Chop up a small selection of the herbs and mix them with ¾ cup of oatmeal and 2 tablespoons of salt.
3. Cut a square piece of cheesecloth big enough to hold some of the mixture.
4. Take the mixture and place it in the cloth. Fold the cloth into a bundle, and then tie the top ends with the string. If you have some of the mixture left over, you can refrigerate it for later use.
5. Using the string, hang the herb-scented bath bag from the faucet in the tub so that the water runs through the bath bag as it fills up the tub.

WRITING UTENSIL CONTAINER

Introduction

Desk drawers are often filled with clutter—namely pens and pencils that roll around every time we open the drawer. Reuse an old metal food can to create a handy container for writing utensils and other items.

Materials:

- Empty large metal food can
- Small piece of decorative paper or wallpaper
- Scissors
- Glue

Directions:

1. Gently remove the label from the can. Then wash and dry the container thoroughly.
2. Cut a piece of decorative paper or wallpaper to match the size of the original label.
3. Cover the back of the paper with glue and then wrap the paper around the can. Press and hold the paper firmly on the can, making sure to smooth out any bubbles.
4. Store your pens, pencils, and markers in the container you have designed!

Glossary

algal bloom a sudden, abnormal explosion of the population of algae in a body of water caused by large amounts of nutrients in the water.

biodegradable easily decomposed by living things.

bisphenol A (BPA) a chemical compound found in some hard plastic items such as baby bottles and reusable plastic drinking bottles.

carbon dioxide a colorless, odorless gas given off by burning and by animals breathing out.

carbon footprint the total amount of carbon dioxide given off by a particular human activity.

carbon offset a credit purchased to release a certain amount of carbon dioxide.

certify to declare something true or correct by an official spoken, written, or printed statement.

chlorine a poisonous gas that is used as a whitener for clothing and paper products. It is also used in cleaning products to disinfect surfaces.

compact fluorescent light bulb (CFL) a small fluorescent light bulb that screws into a standard light socket.

composting the process used to break down yard waste and food scraps into a rich fertilizer for gardens and grass.

conserve to keep from harm or loss; preserve.

conventional farming farming practices that include using human-made chemicals to grow plants.

dead zone an area in the ocean with too little oxygen for plant and animal life to survive.

decompose to break down; decay.

deforestation the destruction of forests.

disinfectant a substance used to destroy germs.

disposable describes items that can be thrown away after use.

electron an extremely tiny particle in atoms that carries a negative charge.

emission an airborne waste product.

Environmental Protection Agency (EPA) the federal agency that works to protect the U.S. environment from pollution.

environmentalist a person who wants to preserve nature and reduce pollution.

European Union (EU) an economic and political group that includes most of the countries of Europe.

evaporate to change from a liquid or solid into a vapor or gas.

fertilizer a substance that helps plants to grow.

filament the metal wire inside of an incandescent light bulb, usually made of tungsten metal.

formaldehyde a colorless gas with a sharp, irritating odor.

fossil fuel underground deposits that were formed millions of years ago from the remains of plants and animals. Coal, oil, and natural gas are fossil fuels.

global warming the gradual warming of Earth's surface, believed by most scientists to be caused by a build-up of greenhouse gases in the atmosphere.

greenhouse effect the process by which certain gases cause the Earth's atmosphere to warm.

greenhouse gas any gas that contributes to the greenhouse effect.

habitat the place where an animal or plant naturally lives or grows.

heavy metal a metal, such as lead, mercury, and arsenic, that can collect in the tissues of organisms and is toxic to most living things.

incandescent light bulb a conventional light bulb that produces more heat than light.

incinerator a waste disposal facility that burns garbage.

integrated pest management (IPM) a natural method of controlling pests and weeds that avoids use of agrochemicals.

landfill a place where trash and other solid waste materials are discarded.

life span the time period from the creation of a material until its destruction.

light-emitting diode (LED) a tiny electrical device that generates light. LED's are highly energy efficient and give off little heat.

monoculture the growth of only one kind of crop.

mulching an agricultural practice that involves covering soil with a layer of such materials as grass clippings, stones, bark chips, and straw.

nonrenewable resources resources that cannot be replenished once depleted, such as fossil fuels.

organic produced by plant or animal activities; organic food is grown or raised without the use of synthetic chemicals.

pesticide a poison that kills pests, such as insects.

petroleum another name for the fossil fuel often called oil.

phosphate a chemical compound found in some dishwasher detergents that can be harmful to water supplies.

pollutant a single source of pollution.

post-consumer waste waste, such as old newspapers and magazines, that has been used by consumers and collected for recycling.

pre-consumer waste waste, such as paper scraps left over from papermaking, that has not come into contact with consumers.

primary battery a battery that stops delivering electric current when its chemicals are expended. Also called a disposable battery.

Processed Chlorine Free (PCF) a label that indicates a paper product is made from recycled content and has been processed without the use of chlorine, although the recycled fibers may have previously been bleached.

recall to take back; withdraw.

reclaimed wood old wood, such as from a demolished building, that is reused to make a new object.

regulate to control by rule, principle, or system.

renewable resource natural resources, such as trees, that can be replaced after they have been harvested.

reproductive having to do with the ways in which organisms copy and perpetuate themselves.

sewage water that contains waste matter produced by human beings.

sustainable any practice that adheres to principles of conservation and ecological balance.

synthetic human-made.

synthetic surfactant a chemical that increases foaming and bubbling during cleaning.

terminal the point on the end of a battery that transfers power to an object.

Totally Chlorine Free (TCF) a label that indicates a paper product was processed without the use of chlorine and is made from virgin wood fibers.

toxin a harmful or poisonous substance.

tungsten-halogen light bulb a quartz bulb that contains tungsten metal and iodine vapor.

ultraviolet rays the invisible rays in the part of the spectrum beyond the violet.

United Nations an international organization that works for world peace and human prosperity.

virgin wood fibers wood fibers used in papermaking that come from newly cut trees.

volatile organic compounds (VOC's) an unstable substance that breaks down over time and gives off small amounts of toxic gases.

Additional Resources

WEB SITES

Connect2Earth
http://www.connect2earth.org

Includes information on environmental issues by topic.

Coop America
http://www.coopamerica.org

Focuses on economic strategies to solve social and environmental problems.

Consumer Reports' Greener Choices
http://www.greenerchoices.org

Contains a wealth of information and helpful tip sheets on green issues and practices.

Envirolink
http://www.envirolink.org/index.html

Includes articles and resources on a range of environmental issues.

Green Living Ideas
http://greenlivingideas.com

Provides numerous articles and information on reducing human impact on the environment.

Green Living Tips
http://www.greenlivingtips.com

Provides tips on how to "green" your lifestyle.

Greenpeace
http://www.greenpeace.org

An organization that works to protect Earth from threats cause by human activity.

National Geographic
http://www.nationalgeographic.com

One of the leading environmental magazines; includes multimedia resources and a student section.

National Geographic Green Guide
http://www.thegreenguide.com/

Includes numerous articles, charts, and tips on greening your lifestyle.

Organic Gardening
http://www.organicgardening.com

A magazine that provides tips to natural, chemical-free gardening.

Sierra Club
http://www.sierraclub.org

A nonprofit organization that works to protect communities and the planet.

TUNZA
http://www.unep.org/Tunza

Part of the United Nations Environment Programme; a student-centered resource for environmental action.

BOOKS

The Green Book: The Everyday Guide to Saving the Earth One Simple Step at a Time by Thomas Kostigen and Elizabeth Rogers (Three Rivers Press, 2007)

Green Guide: The Complete Reference for Consuming Wisely by the Editors of Green Guide (National Geographic, 2008)

It's Easy Being Green: A Handbook for Earth-Friendly Living by Crissy Trask (Gibbs Smith Publishers, 2006)

Living Green: A Practical Guide to Simple Sustainability by Greg Horn (Freedom Press, 2006)

Index

04/09